A **SMITHSONIAN** COLORIN

DINOSAURS

and Other Strange Creatures

Illustrations and text by Peter F. Copeland

Smithsonian Institution Press
Washington, D.C.

Cover: *Ceratosaurus*

Consultants for this book: Nicholas Hotton III, Curator, Department of Paleobiology, National Museum of Natural History, Smithsonian Institution, and Michael K. Brett-Surman, dinosaur specialist and lecturer on dinosaurs at George Washington University

ISBN 0-87474-331-1

01 00 99 98 97 96 8 7 6 5

Printed in the United States of America

Introduction

Dinosaurs roamed over every part of the earth for more than 150 million years. During much of that time, the world in which they lived was a warm, watery place and was covered with great lakes, inland seas, and huge stretches of swampland and marsh.

Dinosaurs were members of the reptile class of animals, as are the snakes, lizards, crocodiles, and turtles of today. The ancestors of dinosaurs were small, fast-running, flesh-eating lizards called thecodonts (THEEK-o-dahnts). These animals moved upright on their hind legs and used their front legs as hands to seize smaller animals, the food on which they lived.

Through millions of years of evolution, dinosaurs gradually developed into a number of very different forms. Some lumbered along with their bodies encased in armored plates of bone, bristling with spikes and horns. Some were the ancestors of birds. Some dinosaurs remained small, but others—plant eaters and flesh eaters alike—grew to be true giants of the earth. A few of these became the largest land animals that have ever lived.

The dinosaurs became extinct about 65 million years ago from a variety of causes. No one is sure exactly why they all disappeared from the earth during one particular time period.

The collection of dinosaur remains (fossils) at the National Museum of Natural History of the Smithsonian Institution is the second largest in the United States and is estimated to be one of the five most extensive collections in the entire world. The new Dinosaur Hall contains a number of specimens never before exhibited. It also represents the most up-to-date scientific thinking on the Age of Dinosaurs.

Dinosaur Colors?

Scientists don't really know what colors the different dinosaurs were, so in coloring these strange creatures, you can give full rein to your imaginations.

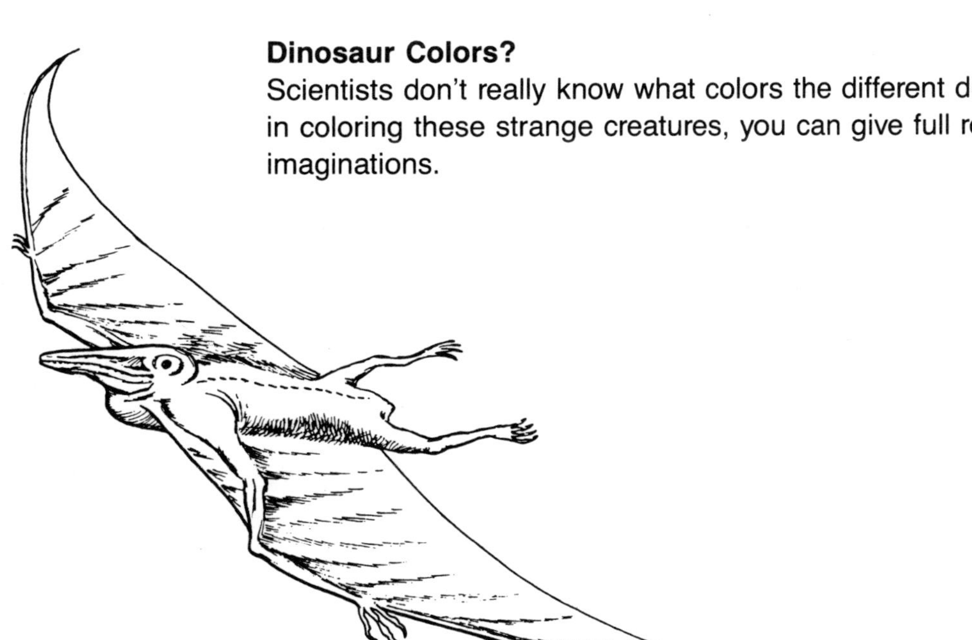

** Two asterisks identify specimens on exhibit in the Dinosaur Hall of the National Museum of Natural History.

* One asterisk identifies specimens in the museum's collection, but which are not currently on public display.

**** Eryops** (AIR-ee-ops) An amphibian (not a reptile) that lived in swamp forests, *Eryops* grew to a length of 6 feet and lived 270 million years ago—before the dinosaurs appeared on the earth.

** **Kannemeyeria** (kan-e-MY-air-ia)

A large plant eater with a great parrotlike beak in place of teeth, *Kannemeyeria* lived in South Africa 200 million years ago alongside the dinosaur ancestors. It sometimes weighed more than a ton.

Ornithosuchus (or-nith-o-SOOK-us) This small, fast-moving, flesh eater was part of the family that gave rise to the dinosaurs. It lived in Europe 210 million years ago.

Coelophysis
(see-lo-FY-sis)

This flesh-eating reptile grew to a length of 10 feet, but was very light in weight because its bones were hollow and thin, like those of a bird. It lived in New Mexico about 200 million years ago.

Dimetrodon (die-MET-row-dahn) ** This fin-backed, flesh-eating reptile, often mistaken for a dinosaur, was in one of the Pelycosaur families and lived in North America 170 million years ago.

Cetiosaurus (set-io-SAWR-us)

This is one of the most ancient of the Sauropods (SAWR-o-pods), plant-eating dinosaurs with long necks and tails, and feet with five toes. Known as the "whale reptile," *Cetiosaurus* was about 50 feet long.

*** Apatosaurus** (a-pat-o-SAWR-us) Once called "Thunder Reptile," this great beast weighed 40 tons and was about 70 feet long. It has sometimes been known as *Brontosaurus* (bront-o-SAWR-us). It lived around rivers in North America, feeding on vegetation, 150 million years ago.

**** Diplodocus** (dip-LAH-doe-kus)

The second longest dinosaur that has been discovered, *Diplodocus* was a plant eater that grew to a length of 80 feet. It lived around rivers 150 million years ago.

** **Brachiosaurus** (brak-io-SAWR-us)

The heaviest land animal that ever lived on earth, this giant plant eater weighed as much as 55 tons. It lived in Africa 150 million years ago.

**** Allosaurus** (al-o-SAWR-us) This fierce, flesh-eating reptile, which grew to a length of more than 30 feet, could kill even the larger dinosaurs. It lived in North America 150 million years ago.

Scelidosaurus
(sel-id-o-SAWR-us)

This dinosaur had a body armed with rows of sharp plates. It was a plant eater, about 13 feet long, and lived about 150 million years ago.

** **Stegosaurus** (steg-o-SAWR-us)

Sharp spikes protected this plated plant eater. Its famous plates were not for protection but acted as "solar-energy" panels. *Stegosaurus* was about 20 feet long and lived about 150 million years ago.

** **Ceratosaurus** (ser-at-o-SAWR-us) A flesh-eating reptile about 17 feet long, *Ceratosaurus* walked on its two powerful hind legs. It lived in North America 150 million years ago.

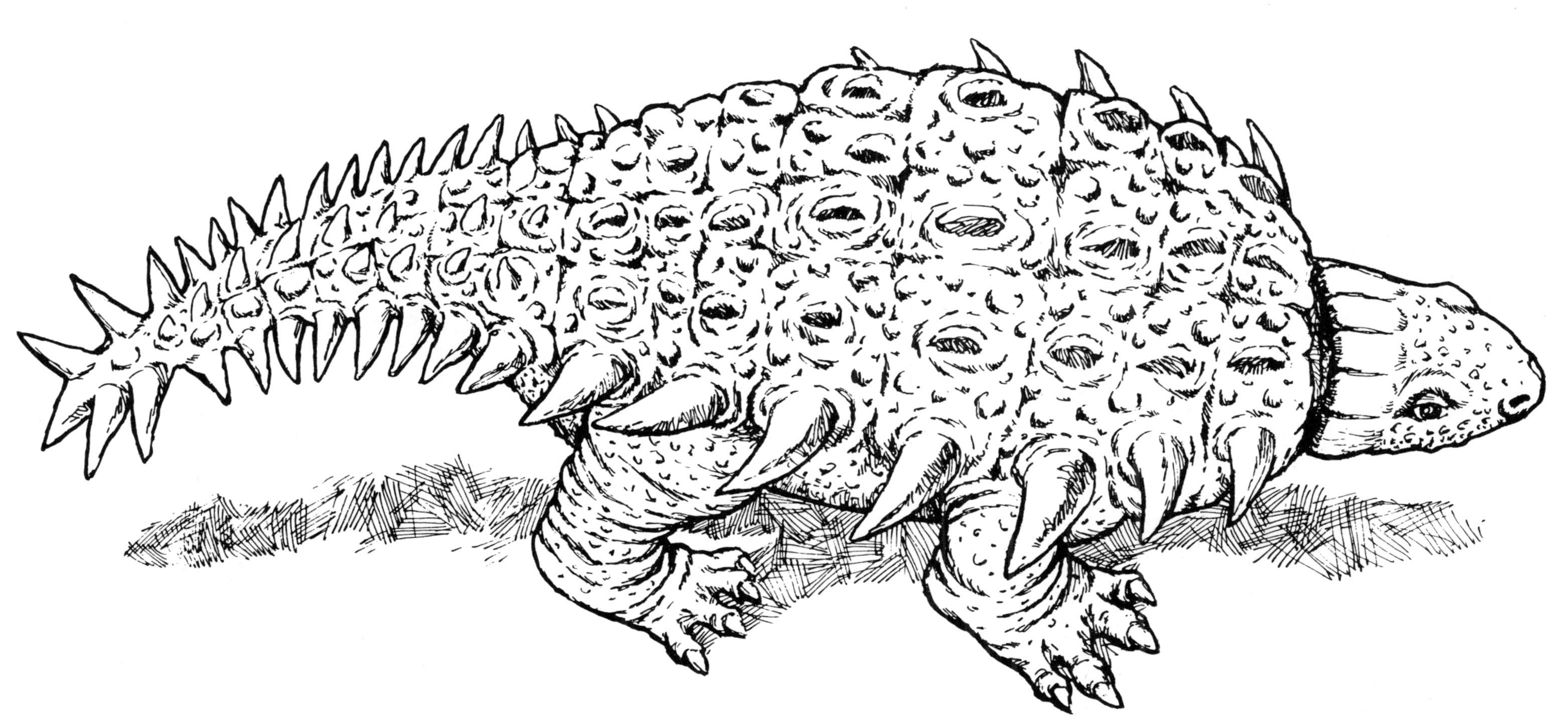

*** Paleoscincus** (pale-eo-SKINK-us) This plant-eating dinosaur, with a completely armored head and sharp spikes along its tail, lived in North America about 150 million years ago.

** **Pterodactylus** (ter-o-DAK-til-us) Another creature often mistaken for a dinosaur, this flying reptile measured less than one foot in length. It lived in Europe 135 million years ago.

*** Iguanodon** (ig-WAN-o-dahn) This plant-eating reptile grew to be 30 feet long and lived in Europe 135 million years ago.

Acanthopholis (a-can-tho-FOE-lis)

Rows of triangular spikes and bony plates ran along the back and tail of this armored reptile. It lived about 135 million years ago.

Hypsilophodon
(hip-sil-oaf-a-dahn)

One of the smallest of the plant-eating dinosaurs, this 5-foot-long reptile lived in Europe about 130 million years ago.

Polacanthus
(pol-ah-CAN-thus)

An armored plant-eating dinosaur about 14 feet long, *Polacanthus* lived in England about 130 million years ago.

Scolosaurus
(skolo-SAWR-us)

Bands of armor much like those of an armadillo protected this plant-eating reptile, which lived in North America about 130 million years ago. It also had a spiked club at the end of its tail.

Spinosaurus
(spine-o-SAWR-us)

The 6-foot-high spiny sail on the back of this big flesh eater was a device that helped the dinosaur keep cool in summer under the hot sun. *Spinosaurus* lived in Egypt 130 million years ago.

* **Protoceratops** (pro-toe-SER-ah-tops) A small dinosaur, measuring only about 6 feet in length, *Protoceratops* had a beak something like that of a parrot and a bony shield that protected its neck. It lived in Mongolia about 100 million years ago.

Gallimimus (gal-ee-MY-mus) This ostrichlike dinosaur, which grew to be 13 feet long, is believed to have dug up and eaten the eggs of other dinosaurs. It lived in Mongolia 90 million years ago.

Phobosuchus (fo-bo-SOOK-us) This monster crocodile, which grew to 50 feet in length, lived in the North American swamps about 90 million years ago.

** **Monoclonius** (mahn-o-CLONE-e-us)

A plant-eating dinosaur, with a horn on its nose like a rhinoceros, *Monoclonius* grew to be 18 feet long. It lived in North America about 80 million years ago.

** **Tyrannosaurus** (tir-an-o-SAWR-us) The biggest flesh-eating land animal that ever lived, this "king of the Tyrant reptiles" had sharp teeth 8 inches long. *Tyrannosaurus* lived in North America 70 million years ago.

**** Triceratops** (try-SERA-tops) This horned plant eater grew to be 24 feet long and lived in North America about 70 million years ago.

**** Corythosaurus** (cor-ith-o-SAWR-us)

A plant eater with a bony crest on top of its head, *Corythosaurus* lived about 70 million years ago. It was about 30 feet long.

**** Edmontosaurus**
(ed-mon-toe-SAWR-us)

This duckbilled, plant-eating dinosaur grew to a length of up to 40 feet and lived in North American swamp forests about 65 million years ago.